ART *for* FUN

Projects

© Aladdin Books Ltd 2001

Designed and produced by
Aladdin Books Ltd
28 Percy Street
London W1P 0LD

First published in the United States in 2001 by
Copper Beech Books,
an imprint of
The Millbrook Press
2 Old New Milford Road
Brookfield, Connecticut 06804

ISBN: 0-7613-2277-9

Editors
Liz White
Leen De Ridder

Concept Design
David West Children's Books

Designer
Flick, Book Design and Graphics

Illustrators
Rob Shone
Catherine Ward - SGA

Cover Design
Liz White

Picture Research
Carlotta Cooper/ Brooks Krikler Research

Printed in the UAE

Cataloging-in-publication data is on file at The Library of Congress

The project editor, Sally Hewitt, is an experienced teacher. She writes and edits books
for children on a wide variety of subjects including art, science, music, and math.

The author, Sue Lacey, is an experienced teacher of art. She currently teaches
elementary school children in England. In her spare time, she paints and sculpts.

photocredits: Abbreviations: t-top, m-middle, b-bottom, r-right, l-left, c-center
Cover, 4b, 5bl, 5tl, 21, 25, 31b, 33, 35, 39, 41, 43, 45, 49, 51, 53, 55b, 59, 61, 62, 65, 66, 69, 73, 75, 81,
83, 85, 96, 103b, 117, 126tl, 127l, 128b : AKG London. 9b, 10, 11b, 15, 27, 29, 104, 107, 111, 125:
AKG/ Erich Lessing. 5tr, 13, 95, 109: AKG ©Succession Picasso/ DACS 1999. 16b: Musée
Marmottan. 23, 119: AKG ©DACS 1999. 3c, 34, 37, 44, 80, 84, 91, 92, 97: Roger Vlitos. 46, 89, 99:
AKG © ADAGP, Paris and DACS, London 2000. 5mr, 5br, 70: the Musée Picasso, Paris © Succession
Picasso. 76: AKG © Salvador Dali — Foundation Gala — Salvador Dali/ DACS 2000. 90, 115:
Reproduced by permission of the Henry Moore Foundation. 79b, 101, 113: Frank Spooner Pictures.
121: James Davis Travel Photography. 122: Tate Gallery Publications © Estate of Gwen John 1999.

10 9 8 7 6 5 4 3 2

ART *for* FUN
Projects

Sue Lacey

COPPER BEECH BOOKS
BROOKFIELD • CONNECTICUT

INTRODUCTION

Artists work with many different tools and materials to make art. They also spend a lot of time looking carefully at shapes, patterns, and colors.

This book is about how artists see the world around them. On every page you will find a work of art by a different famous artist, which will give you ideas and inspiration for the project.

You don't have to be a brilliant artist to do the projects. Look at each piece of art, learn about the artists, and have fun being creative.

CONTENTS

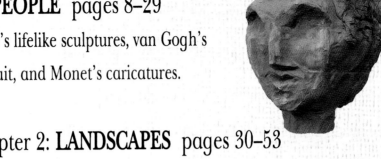

WORKING LIKE AN ARTIST

It can help you in your work if you start by looking carefully and collecting ideas, just like an artist. Artists usually carry a sketchbook around with them all the time so they can get their ideas on paper right away.

Words
You can write some words to remind you of the shapes, colors, and patterns you see

Materials
Try out different pencils, pens, paints, pastels, crayons, and materials to see what they do. Which would be the best for this work?

Color
When you use color, mix all the colors you want first and try them out. It is amazing how many different colors you can make.

Using a sketchbook

Before you start each project, a sketchbook is the place to do your sketches. Try out your tools and materials, mix colors, and stick in some interesting papers and fabrics. You can then choose which you want to use.

Be a magpie

Make a collection of things that are of interest to you like feathers, stones, or materials. Anything that catches your eye could be useful in your artwork.

Art box You can collect tools and materials together for your work and put them in a box. Sometimes you may need to go to an art store to buy exactly what you need. Often you can find things at home you can use. Ask for something for your art box for your next birthday!

CHAPTER 1: PEOPLE

CONTENTS

In this chapter you can look at how artists see people. Some artists like to draw or paint in a way that makes their subject look as lifelike as possible. Others find it more important to express a certain feeling or emotion in their piece of art.

See which artists you like, and try their styles to make a sculpture or painting of your friends and family. You can also look in the mirror and make a self-portrait!

Drawing people

Drawing people is easier if you can get the proportions right. Remember always to look carefully.

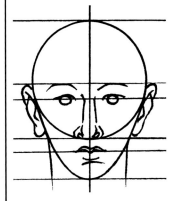

Head shape
Look at the shape and draw the outline. Practice drawing eyes, noses, mouths, and ears in your sketchbook. How will you do the hair?

Face measurements
It helps when drawing a face to divide the head into sections as shown. See how the eyes sit on one line, and the nose on another. Look at where the ears and mouth are.

Body measurements
About six heads fit into a full-length body. So, whatever size you draw the head, measure two more to the waist and three more to the feet.

Always sketch first, and draw in the details afterward.

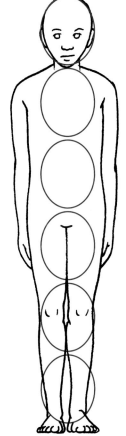

PAINTING ON A SURFACE

WHAT YOU NEED
Clay • Rolling Pin
Pencils • Paints
Felt-tip Pen

Rekhmere was an Egyptian court official. He wanted his tomb full of pictures of his life. What picture would remind you of home? You could paint a picture of your life on clay. Make sure the people are facing sideways.

PROJECT: PAINTING ON A CLAY SURFACE

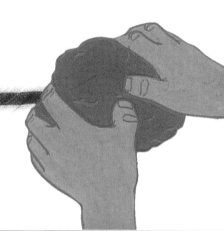

Step 1. Take a lump of clay and knead it with your hands to make it soft.

GALLERY

Tomb of Rekhmere, Court Official 15th Century B.C.
THEBES NEW KINGDOM 18TH DYNASTY

MESSAGES

Messages were put on the wall using word pictures, called hieroglyphics, which was Egyptian writing.

SIDE VIEWS

Look at the people facing sideways. This is how Egyptian artists drew people.

Step 2. Roll out the clay. Don't worry if the edges are not square.

Step 3. While the clay is drying, look at the Egyptian art. When the clay is dry, sketch a picture of you and your family onto it. Make the people face sideways the way they did in Egyptian art.

Step 4. Use paints to color your clay art. You can darken the outlines with felt-tip pen.

Important ancient Egyptians like Rekhmere used to build their tombs before they died. Artists would paint the walls with wonderful pictures to help make the dead feel at home in the afterlife. This painting shows some craftsmen at work carving wood for Rekhmere.

WHAT YOU NEED
Balloon • Tape
Cardboard Tube
Flour • Water
Newspaper
Paintbrush • Paints

WORKING IN 3-D

Sculpture is three-dimensional, or 3-D, which means that it can be looked at from every side. Do some sketches of a friend like Picasso did. You can use your sketches to help you make a papier-mâché model to look like your friend.

PROJECT: SCULPTURE OF A HEAD

Step 1. You can make a 3-D head by using a balloon, a tube, and some papier-mâché. Blow up the balloon and tape it on top of the tube.

Step 2. Mix some flour and water into a soggy paste. Tear old newspapers into strips, dip them in the paste, and cover the balloon with two layers of paper.

Step 3. Make a nose, eyes, ears, and mouth by crumpling and molding newspaper into shapes and pasting them onto the balloon. Don't forget the hair. Wait for it to dry before you paint it. You could use a bronze color, or bright colors if you prefer.

GALLERY

Head of Dora Maar 1942
PABLO PICASSO (1881 – 1973)

MODELS
Picasso used to ask his friends to sit for him while he drew them and made sculptures of their heads.

SURFACE
Can you see all the different marks on the face and hair, made by the tools Picasso used?

METHOD
Look at the simple lines and shapes Picasso used to make this sculpture of Dora Maar.

MATERIALS
The head was made in clay first to get all the shapes and details right.

The Spanish artist Pablo Picasso changed the way people saw art because he made unusual and very different paintings, drawings, pottery, and sculpture. He did not want his art to look like a photograph. Picasso used his imagination to make art in a way that no one else had ever done.

PATTERN AND COLOR

WHAT YOU NEED
Cardboard • Tape
Pen • Colored
Tissue • Paper
Candy Wrappers
Shiny Paper • Yarn
String • Any Fabrics,
Papers, or Materials

You can make a figure using patterns and colors. Add some gold and silver paper, and paint, and make it in the style of Klimt. It would be fun to cover a life-sized picture in different fabrics, papers, and materials.

PROJECT: A LIFE-SIZED FIGURE

Step 1. Collect pieces of cardboard, and tape them together to make them as long as your friend. Draw around your friend with a pen. Use large pieces of bright-colored tissue paper to decorate the background.

Step 2. Look at Klimt's lovely patterns and shapes and copy some. Glue some candy wrappers or bright fabrics to make the clothes.

Step 3. You can use pictures of faces from magazines for the face. Yarn or string will make good hair.

GALLERY

The Kiss 1908
GUSTAV KLIMT (1862 – 1918)

GOLD
Klimt's father made gold objects. Klimt used to watch him work and liked to make gold an important part of his own artwork.

MOSAIC
After seeing mosaics in Italy, Klimt made this carpet of flowers look like a mosaic.

MODEL
The woman's face looks like the wife of one of Klimt's close friends.

PATTERN
Can you see the different types of pattern on the man's and woman's clothes?

Many people in Austria, where Gustav Klimt lived, thought he was an unusual and interesting artist. He was a big, quiet man who worked hard in his studio from early morning to late evening. All his paintings had a great deal of pattern in them. He used straight lines for men and curved shapes for women. Hands interested him, and he often made them an important part of his pictures.

CARICATURES

WHAT YOU NEED
Pencils • Paper
Sketchbook

Drawing was Monet's best subject at school. He found other schoolwork boring, but drew caricatures of his schoolteachers and friends to amuse them. Caricatures are often drawn of famous people to make fun of them, but you can do yours for enjoyment!

GALLERY

Caricatures c.1855
CLAUDE MONET (1840 – 1926)

CARICATURE
A caricature is made when an artist takes a person's features and exaggerates them.

HEAD AND BODY
Sometimes Monet would give his caricature a small body. This would make the head look even more unusual.

PROJECT: DRAWING A CARICATURE

Step 1. Once you have made your sketch or chosen a photograph, look at it carefully and pick out some special features, like the nose, eyes, hairstyle, or chin.

Step 2. Practice enlarging and changing them in your sketchbook so they look amusing (but not unkind!)

Claude Monet always enjoyed drawing when he was at school in France. This is when he started to draw caricatures. He also liked to paint outdoors. He traveled a great deal, always taking his paints with him. Later, Monet became part of a group of French painters called Impressionists. He used paint to capture the way light played on landscapes and buildings.

Step 3. Choose what you are going to exaggerate and then draw the caricature. Can you still tell who it is meant to be? You can add a small body like Monet did if you like.

CARVING

Michelangelo used to travel to a quarry to choose pieces of marble for his sculptures. Carvings can be made from many different materials, including soap. It is soft to cut and easy to find at home.

PROJECT: CARVING A SOAP HEAD

Step 1. You will need some plastic modeling tools, but an old nail file, orange stick, or plastic knife will do as well. Work on a piece of newspaper so you do not make too much mess.

Step 2. Mark where you will put the eyes, nose, mouth, and hair on the soap, using a pointed tool. Start to carve out the shapes until the soap looks like a face (see tips on page 7).

Step 3. Add the details like eyebrows, hair, and cheeks. You could make faces of all your family in different colors, and display them in the bathroom!

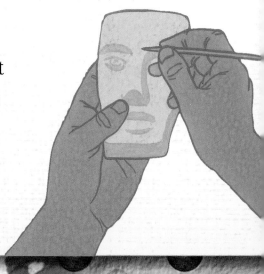

18

GALLERY

The Madonna of the Stairs 1491–1492
MICHELANGELO BUONARROTI (1475 – 1564)

MATERIALS
This picture of the Virgin Mary and her baby Jesus was carved from a slab of marble only 2 inches thick.

YOUNG ARTIST
Michelangelo carved this when he was sixteen. He has made the Virgin Mary and Jesus look like an ordinary mother and baby.

LOW RELIEF
The figures are cut just slightly into the surface of the marble, using a fine chisel. This method of work is called low relief.

CARVING
Although carved out of solid marble, the clothes flow as if they are real.

By the time he was thirteen, Michelangelo had begun to learn to paint and make sculpture. A great deal of his work was for the Christian church and showed scenes from the Bible. His most famous painting is on the ceiling of the Sistine Chapel in Rome, which he painted all by himself.

SELF-PORTRAITS

WHAT YOU NEED
Pencil • Thick Paper
Acrylic Paints
Palette • Brushes
Glue Spreader
Corrugated
Cardboard

Look carefully at van Gogh's self-portrait, then try out some swirls and lines of your own. Mix the paint thickly and put it on the page using a strip of cardboard or a glue spreader. Get as much texture into your portrait as possible.

PROJECT: TEXTURE

Step 1. Look at yourself in a mirror. Draw your head and shoulders on a piece of cardboard or thick paper.

Step 2. Start painting, using acrylic paint and a variety of tools. Use a glue spreader, corrugated cardboard, and brushes. You can even squeeze the paint straight from the tube! Make the paint really thick.

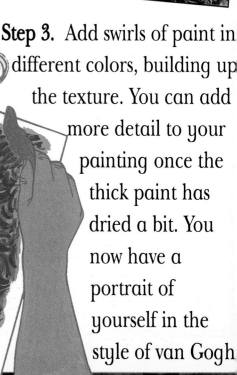

Step 3. Add swirls of paint in different colors, building up the texture. You can add more detail to your painting once the thick paint has dried a bit. You now have a portrait of yourself in the style of van Gogh

GALLERY

Self-Portrait 1889
VINCENT VAN GOGH (1853 – 1890)

SHADING
To show light and dark on the painting, van Gogh used shades of blue and green.

COLOR
You can see that a mixture of blues, greens, and white have been used in this picture. Van Gogh chose colors to fit his mood. How do you think he was feeling?

BRUSH STROKES
Look closely at the background and you will see a swirly pattern. There are also curved and straight lines on van Gogh's jacket and face.

THICK PAINT
Van Gogh used very thick oil paint. He put it on the canvas with big brush strokes.

Vincent van Gogh grew up in Holland but later lived and worked on his paintings in France. When he was thirty-six, he painted this portrait of himself looking like a French farmer. Van Gogh did not want to paint like anyone else, and nobody seemed to understand his way of working.

ABSTRACT PORTRAITS

WHAT YOU NEED
Paper • Pens
Pencils • Ruler
Crayons • Chalks
Paints

Paul Klee's painting is abstract rather than realistic. He used geometric shapes like circles, ovals, triangles, rectangles, and squares to make his portrait. You can draw a picture of people you know in the same style.

PROJECT: ARRANGING SHAPES

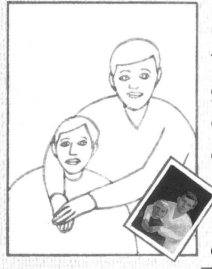

Step 1. Look at what you are going to draw and decide how you could divide it into geometric shapes. Draw in the body and head shapes as a starting point.

Step 2. Draw in shapes across and around the people. Use curved and straight lines and many different shapes.

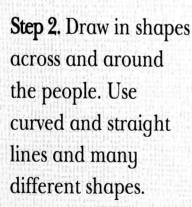

Step 3. Choose some colors that you think will give the portraits life and character. You can use pencils, crayons, chalks, or paints to color in your drawing.

22

GALLERY

Senecio 1922
PAUL KLEE (1879 – 1940)

SIMPLE SHAPES
Can you see how this face is made up of simple rectangles, squares, triangles, and circles?

COLOR
Each shape and color is carefully chosen to give the face expression and make it come alive.

TEXTURE
Klee painted this picture on linen, which is a roughly woven material. You can see the texture of the cloth through the paint.

Paul Klee did not paint like other artists of his day. He liked to work alone and usually did about two hundred pictures a year, each one different from the last. Many of his pictures were made up of shapes and patterns that had a hidden meaning. This portrait is called *Senecio*, which is the name of a group of plants. The title is the clue to help us see that Klee has painted this face to look like the head of a flower.

MAKING A MOSAIC

Look at the colors, patterns, and tones in this mosaic from Ravenna in Italy. It was made by pressing pieces of colored glass, marble, and stone into cement to make a large picture. You can make your own mosaic using paper.

PROJECT: MOSAIC PORTRAIT

Step 1. Find a picture in a magazine or a photo of a friend. Draw an outline of the face on a piece of cardboard.

Step 2. Cut or tear lots of colored scraps of paper from magazines. Choose colors that you can use to create a face, mouth, eyes, nose, and hair. Try to find lots of different tones of the same color.

Step 3. Glue the scraps to the cardboard to build up the face. When it is dry, paint over it with craft glue mixed with water as a varnish.

GALLERY

The Empress Theodora with Her Retinue C.547
RAVENNA, ITALY

COLOR
Look at the wonderfully rich colors used for this mosaic. Small pieces of bright glass were the main material used.

MATERIALS
Semiprecious stones were used in the mosaic to make Empress Theodora's beautiful jewelry.

PATTERNS
How many different patterns are there? They show how important she was.

DETAIL
Many pieces were used to create each face. They are so well done that from a distance they look like a painting.

This mosaic is almost fifteen hundred years old. Many churches used mosaics to tell Bible stories. The artist for this mosaic is unknown, but the mosaics in Ravenna are probably the most famous in the world. This one shows the Roman Empress Theodora bringing gifts to the church.

ASSEMBLAGE

WHAT YOU NEED
A Collection of
Interesting Objects
Cardboard • Pencils
Craft Glue • String

Many famous people liked Arcimboldo's portraits so much that they paid him to paint one for them. Arcimboldo's paintings are made by assembling a collection of objects. You can make a strange head using things you have at home.

PROJECT: COLLAGE

Step 1. Collect all kinds of interesting objects like paper clips, thread spools, string, nuts and bolts, hooks, screws, pins, wire, wrappers, and wood. Find a piece of cardboard from an old box. It will need to be thick and fairly big. Glue on some fine string to make the outline of a face and neck.

Step 2. Try out different objects you have collected to see which look best as eyes, ears, nose, and mouth. Choose something that would make good hair. When you have made your arrangement, glue it in place and let it dry. You could frame it and invite your friends to see your curious picture.

GALLERY

Vertumnus 1590
GIUSEPPE ARCIMBOLDO (1527 – 1593)

FRUIT
Can you see why each piece of fruit has been chosen? The pear looks like the shape of a nose.

MATERIALS
What would you choose to make a head, eyes, nose, mouth, and hair if you were to make a picture like Arcimboldo's?

DETAIL
Each fruit and flower is painted with great care, showing every detail. Some look good enough to eat.

SUBJECT
Do you find this man's head interesting, friendly, or a bit frightening?

An Italian, born in 1527, Arcimboldo started his work as an artist by making stained-glass windows for churches. He became interested in painting strange and curious people who were considered grotesque. He painted fruit, flowers, trees, and vegetables to create his amazing heads.

USE OF COLOR

WHAT YOU NEED
Paper • Pencil
Tracing Paper
Paints
Paintbrush

Berthe Morisot used cool colors to create a peaceful mood. In your sketchbook, try mixing warm reds, yellows, purples, and oranges as well as cool greens, blues, grays, and lavenders. You can use them to create different moods in your work.

PROJECT: WARM AND COOL COLORS

Step 1. Draw a picture of something you enjoy doing. Trace it and make an exact copy on a piece of paper the same size. Paint one picture using only warm colors.

Step 2. Paint the second picture using only cool colors and see how different the two pictures look. How do the colors make you feel? Which one do you prefer?

GALLERY

The Cradle 1872
BERTHE MORISOT (1841 – 1895)

COLORS
Most of the colors used by Morisot are cool blues, grays, greens, and whites. They create a sense of peace and quiet, just right for the baby.

SHADING
The woman is Edma, Berthe's sister. The loving mother with her black hair and dark clothes, quietly looking at her baby asleep, draws your eye toward the baby in the cradle.

LIGHT
The dark background makes the light cradle stand out.

Women were not allowed to study art in college when Berthe Morisot lived in France. Berthe and her sister Edma were determined to learn to paint, so their father allowed them to have lessons. Berthe had a free and easy style, putting the paint on the canvas so you could see the different brush strokes and colors.

CHAPTER 2: LANDSCAPES

CONTENTS

When learning to paint or draw landscapes, it is a good idea to make a sketch first. Next, experiment with different paints and brushes, or even with your fingers!

Try to look carefully at the effects of the light when you are outside. On an overcast day a landscape will look different than it does on a sunny day.

Look at how different artists create landscapes and have fun making one yourself!

Drawing landscapes

When learning to draw and paint landscapes, there are some simple techniques that can help you to improve your skills.

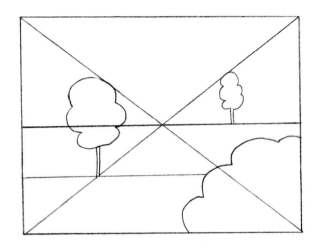

Composition

A landscape has things in the foreground, the middle ground, and the distance. Above is a simple grid that will help you with composition.

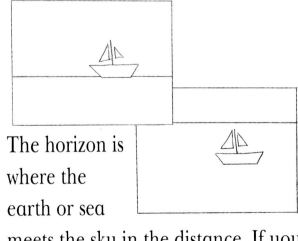

The horizon is where the earth or sea meets the sky in the distance. If you move the horizon line on a painting, you can make the same landscape or seascape look very different.

SEEING LIGHT

Many of Monet's paintings show the same landscapes at different times of the day. Look at some trees near where you live and see how they change color as the light changes. Make some sketches of the trees and paint them in Monet's colors.

PROJECT: PAINTING LIGHT

Step 1. Draw some trees near your home in your sketchbook. Look carefully at the shape of the trunk, branches, and leaves.

Step 2. Mix as many different blues and yellows as you can. Try them out in your sketchbook. Paint the trees using the colors you have mixed. Make dabs, blobs, and lines of color next to each other. For white, let the white paper show through.

Step 3. Try painting the same trees at different times of the day and different times of the year like Monet. See how the colors change.

GALLERY

The Three Poplars, Fall 1891
CLAUDE MONET (1840-1926)

CONTRAST
The trees stand out against the sky because the blue, gold, and pink contrast with each other.

DISTANCE
The trees and sky in the distance are very pale, which makes them look farther away.

SEASONS
This painting shows poplar trees in the fall. Monet painted the same trees in the spring and summer.

BRUSHSTROKES
Monet put dabs and lines of different colors near each other. They give the painting texture.

Claude Monet had a hard time when he set out to become an artist. His family would not give him any money, and his wife died when she was young. He worked outside using many colors to show how landscapes were altered by the ever-changing light. At first, nobody liked his pictures, but later people bought his paintings and he became rich.

COMPOSITION AND COLOR

WHAT YOU NEED
Small Box • Paint
Paintbrushes
Cardboard
Pencil • Pens
Watercolor Paint
Glue or Tape
Scissors

The way a picture is put together is called its composition. You can make the foreground and middle ground stand out from the background in a 3-D composition.

PROJECT: 3-D COMPOSITION

Step 1. Take a small box and paint an ocean on the bottom and halfway up the inside. The rest can be the sky. Look at Cézanne's painting to help you with colors.

Step 3. Make a frame for the front of the box and draw and paint trees on it. Glue it to the front of the box. You now have a 3-D painting.

Step 2. You may need help with this. Cut a piece of cardboard slightly smaller than the front of the box. Draw some houses and trees in pencil. Paint with watercolor. Cut around the top edge. Fold the bottom under and glue or tape it into the box halfway in.

GALLERY

La Mer à L'Estaque 1883-1886
PAUL CÉZANNE (1839-1906)

COMPOSITION
Can you see how the painting is divided into three: the foreground, which is trees and land, the middle ground, which is the houses, and the ocean and mountains in the background.

DISTANCE
The foreground shows the most detail. Paler colors have been used to paint the sky and mountains. It makes them seem farther in the distance.

Paul Cézanne grew up in southern France. He was a shy, awkward young man who longed to be a painter. After working for a while in his father's bank, Cézanne went to Paris to become an artist. Through copying the work of famous artists, he taught himself to paint. Working outside was important to Cézanne, and he made up a new way of painting using blocks of color. Later he was called the "Father of Modern Art," because of his original style.

MOVEMENT

WHAT YOU NEED
Cardboard • Pencils
Acrylic Paints
Paintbrush • Comb

Vincent van Gogh used very thick oil paint to bring his paintings to life. You can use acrylic paints, which dry more quickly. If you mix your paints very thickly, you can paint a sky with swirls of color like van Gogh's.

GALLERY

The Starry Night 1889
VINCENT VAN GOGH (1853-1890)

CONTRAST
The dark cypress tree stands out against the light of the stars in the evening sky.

SKIES
"I never get tired of looking at the blue sky," van Gogh told his mother. Here he has painted a glowing night sky.

FEELING
Van Gogh put a great deal of feeling into his work. If you look closely, you can see almost every line of paint.

PROJECT: MOVEMENT IN PAINTING

Step 1. On a piece of cardboard, sketch the sky, some trees, and plants on a starry, moonlit night. Don't forget the shadows.

Step 2. Mix some blues, purples, black, yellows, and white. Make sure the paint is really thick. Start at the top of your sketch and paint the shapes with lines and swirls of blue, purple, and yellow. A comb can be used to add texture.

During his life, Vincent van Gogh was poor, often hungry and ill — he was rejected by many people. The church did not want his help with the poor. Artists did not like his paintings. His brother Theo was the only person who believed in him. Van Gogh had very little money while he was alive, but after his death his paintings began to sell for thousands, or even millions, of dollars.

Step 3. When the paint has almost dried, add some circles and swirls of white and yellow for the stars and the moon.

MIXING COLOR

Seurat used lots of colored dots to build up a picture. With a matchstick, experiment in your sketchbook with little dots of acrylic paint. Try to make an ocean, sky, and land look different from each other through the colors.

PROJECT: POINTILLISM

Step 1. Draw a simple ocean scene in pencil. Make sure it isn't too big!

Step 2. Put some red, yellow, and blue acrylic paint on a paper plate. It's better to use a different matchstick for each color.

Step 3. Dip them into the paint and build up your picture using lots of colored dots. If you want to make a green area, you could mix blue dots and yellow dots. How do you think you could make an orange area?

WHAT YOU NEED
Pencil • Paper Plate
Acrylic Paint • Paper
Used Matchstick

GALLERY

Port-en-Bessin 1888
GEORGES SEURAT (1859-1891)

OBSERVATION
Try using a magnifying glass to look at the colors.

FEELING
One of Seurat's aims was to give a great deal of feeling to his work. What do you feel when you look at this picture?

REPETITION
Seurat painted this French port over and over again. Each painting looks very different.

LIGHT AND SPACE
Seurat used pale colored dots to give a sense of light and space.

Young Georges Seurat lived in Paris where his mother and uncle taught him to paint and draw. Seurat then decided to spend the rest of his life painting. He started a whole new way of working called "pointillism." He would put different colored dots of paint next to each other to build up a whole picture. Many summers were spent by the sea painting the same view, especially at Port-en-Bessin.

COLORS AND SHAPES

WHAT YOU NEED
Paint • Paintbrush
Cardboard • Pencils
Scissors • Glue
Paper

Gauguin used bright colors and simple shapes in his paintings. Look at a small part of Gauguin's painting and examine the colors and shapes he used. You can make a wonderful collage using the same style.

PROJECT: ABSTRACT COLLAGE

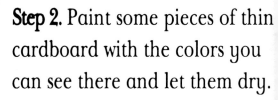

Step 1. Make a viewfinder by folding a piece of paper into four. Cut out the middle and open it out. Put it over the part of Gauguin's painting (opposite) that you like the best.

Step 2. Paint some pieces of thin cardboard with the colors you can see there and let them dry.

Step 3. Lightly draw each shape in your viewfinder onto the right color of cardboard and cut them out.

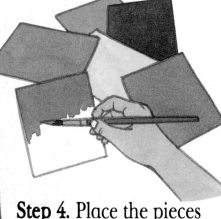

Step 4. Place the pieces onto a larger piece of cardboard. Glue them down when you are happy with the arrangement.

GALLERY

Matamoe 1892
PAUL GAUGUIN (1848-1903)

COLOR
What mood do you think Gauguin was trying to show in this painting with the colors he used?

SHAPE
Look at the way Gauguin has made the shapes in his picture very simple

DETAIL
How many things can you see that have been painted in their exact color?

Paul Gauguin led a life as colorful as his paintings. He often worked with van Gogh and other famous painters. He left French society and traveled to the South Seas to fulfill himself as an artist. Gauguin thought that light, shape, and color were the most important part of paintings. You can see this in his work and in the moods that he creates in his paintings.

WEATHER AND SKIES

The sky often changes color with the weather. Constable would sometimes use the skies in his paintings to reflect his mood. You could experiment with pastels and colors to create your own sky scene.

PROJECT: PASTEL SKIES

Step 1. Try out pastels in your sketchbook to see how they work. Apply them in layers and use your fingers to smudge them, or let the paper show through. Spray the finished work with hairspray (to fix the pastels.)

Step 2. Look out of a window, or sit outside at different times, to make a number of sketches of the sky. Look for grays, yellows, reds, oranges, and white, not just blue! Try to include some unusual features; sunsets, rainbows, or storm clouds are interesting.

GALLERY

River Landscape c1820
JOHN CONSTABLE (1776-1837)

SKIES
Constable thought skies were one of the most important parts of his paintings.

SKETCHES
Constable made many sketches in charcoal or paint before he started a painting.

John Constable loved the English countryside, he spent most of his life there. He wanted to express his love of the countryside through his art. He would find a beautiful view and sit and sketch in charcoal and paint for hours. He loved to paint the clouds he saw as the weather changed.

SEASCAPES

Turner used white with oil to make his paint look almost transparent. He also liked to create a texture on the surface. If you use glue, tissue paper, and paint, you can get a transparent, textured effect to your work.

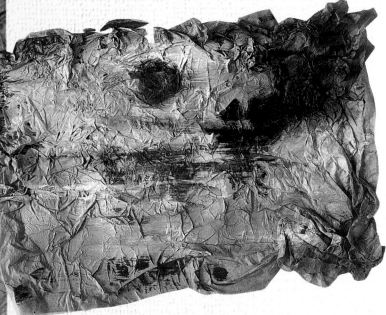

PROJECT: MIXED MEDIA

Step 2. Mix different yellow, red, orange, and white colors for a sea picture. Use a big, soft brush to paint on top of the tissue paper making waves and swirls of water. Use lots of different colors like Turner. Let them blend into each other.

Step 1. Put some glue on the cardboard. Crease and crumple some plain tissue paper and lay it on the cardboard. Paint more glue over the textured surface and leave it to dry.

GALLERY

The *Sun of Venice* Setting Sail 1843
J.M.W. TURNER (1775-1851)

PALETTE KNIFE
Instead of using a brush, Turner used a small, flat knife to spread the oil paint on the canvas.

POETRY
This painting tells a sad story Turner read in a poem. It was about a fishing boat leaving Venice, never to return because of storms.

CONTRAST
The darker ripples of the sea contrast with the white and yellow sky.

The first drawings Turner did were put in the window of his father's barbershop in Covent Garden, London. At 14 he began to study art seriously and had his first picture in an art gallery when he was 17. As he traveled around England and Europe, he filled hundreds of sketchbooks with wonderful drawings and sketches, which he later turned into paintings.

SEEING SHAPES

Kandinsky worked in paint. He used large areas of solid color to make shapes. You can use the same ideas to make a textile landscape. Choose bright colors like the ones in the Murnau landscape, and glue and stitch them to some material.

GALLERY

Landscape with Church I 1909
WASSILY KANDINSKY (1866-1944)

PROJECT: TEXTILES

Step 1. Collect some brightly colored material. You need a large piece of heavy fabric as a background. Cut out some shapes like the ones in Kandinsky's painting.

Step 2. Arrange your material on the background to make a picture. Glue the pieces in place. Once the glue has dried, add some stitches to the materials in colored thread for small interesting features like stars, leaves, or windows.

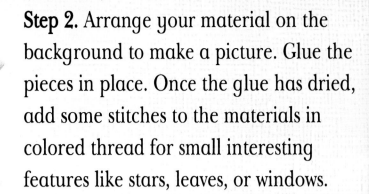

COLOR
This landscape is painted in patches of bright color. How many different colors can you see? Each color plays an important part in creating an atmosphere or mood in this work of art.

FRIENDSHIP
Kandinsky did many paintings while he was staying at his friend's vacation home at Murnau.

FOCAL POINT
An important part of a painting that draws your eye is called the focal point. What do you think is the focal point of this picture?

Dr. Wassily Kandinsky was all set to become a university professor in Russia when he decided he wanted to study art. He went on to paint in many different and exciting modern styles. He loved modern music and thought that as different sounds made a whole piece of music, so different colors and shapes can come together to make a painting.

LIGHT AND COLOR

WHAT YOU NEED
Acrylic Paints
Paper Plate
Cardboard
Paintbrush or
Garden Stake
Old Rag

Renoir's painting has a sense of life and movement. A brush is not the only tool that can be used with paint. Artists often use their fingers and the end of their brushes to give texture and a feeling of movement.

PROJECT: FINGER PAINTING

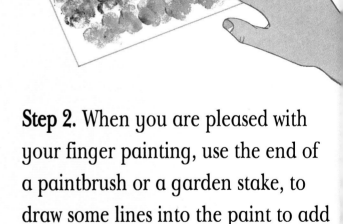

Step 1. Collect some colored acrylic paints and put them on a paper plate. Use your finger to spread the paint on a piece of cardboard. Wash your finger and dry it on a rag before using another color! Try using dabs and strokes to create water, sky, and land.

Step 2. When you are pleased with your finger painting, use the end of a paintbrush or a garden stake, to draw some lines into the paint to add to the texture.

GALLERY

The Seine at Champrosay 1876
PIERRE AUGUSTE RENOIR (1841-1919)

LIGHT
Renoir has chosen colors that make his painting full of light.

COLOR
Blue, green, and white are cool colors. Renoir has used them to paint this seascape.

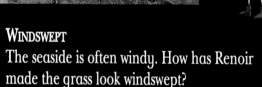

HAPPINESS
How does this painting seem a happy and not a sad picture?

WINDSWEPT
The seaside is often windy. How has Renoir made the grass look windswept?

When he was 13, Auguste Renoir worked in a factory in France, painting flowers onto china cups and saucers. This was the start of his love of painting. Later, Monet became his friend, and together they sat outside painting the shimmering light on water, trees, and hills. Renoir wanted every painting he did to be full of happiness.

JAPANESE ART

Hokusai used to paint, but he also used to make prints by carving a picture in wood and printing from it. You can draw a landscape in Hokusai's style and make a print from it using a flat piece of polystyrene called a press-print sheet.

PROJECT: BRIDGE PRINT

Step 1. Design a picture of a bridge going over a river or road. Using a pencil, draw it into the press-print sheet.

Step 2. Cover the sheet with one color of printing ink— blue or black would look good. Press it onto a sheet of paper. Carefully peel back the paper. Do several prints until you get the best one.

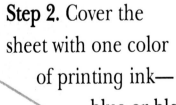

GALLERY

The Bridge in Fuji, c1820
KATSUSHIKA HOKUSAI (1760-1849)

MOUNT FUJI
Can you see Mount Fuji in the distance?

LINES
Look at all the different lines in this print. They are very fine and crisp.

SHADOWS
Hokusai did not put shadows in his landscapes. This makes them look very flat and suitable for making a print.

SKYLINE
Most Japanese landscapes have a thin, blue line for the sky.

One of Japan's most famous artists, Hokusai, started his career as an artist by making prints from blocks of wood. He was adopted by a family in Tokyo, and they helped him train as an artist. He painted, printed, and illustrated books. He was particularly interested in bridges, and did many bridge prints and paintings during his long life.

SKETCHING

WHAT YOU NEED
Charcoal • Paper
Eraser

Morisot would often sketch a landscape before painting it. She would look carefully at the scene first. Charcoal is good to use for sketching as it can smudge, it can be dark or light, and an eraser can make interesting marks on it.

PROJECT: CHARCOAL SKETCH

Step 1. Choose a scene you would like to sketch. Try out some different marks you can make with the charcoal.

Step 2. Lightly draw in the outlines of the different shapes you see. Darken the areas that are in shadow and smudge the charcoal to make lighter shapes. Add details.

Step 3. If you want to lighten some areas, use an eraser to take away some charcoal and let the paper show through.

GALLERY

In the Cornfield at Gennevilliers 1875
BERTHE MORISOT (1841-1895)

MOOD
Look at the colors Morisot uses. How do they make you feel?

LOOSE STYLE
Most of Morisot's work has a free and easy look to the way the paint is put on the canvas.

DIARY
Berthe's paintings were like a diary of good times spent with family and friends.

SKETCHES
Before painting, Morisot would make pencil or charcoal sketches.

The first time Berthe Morisot had an art lesson was to help her draw a birthday card for her father. She went on to become an important member of the group of artists called French Impressionists. Berthe painted everyday scenes of her own family life and spent a great deal of time with the artist Renoir when he painted outside.

CHAPTER 3: SPORTS AND LEISURE

CONTENTS

What is your favorite sport? What do you like doing in your leisure time?

In the past, before there were televisions, computers, and movies, people had very different ways of spending their leisure time. They would go on picnics, sit in cafés to talk to their friends, or perhaps go on boat trips. You can see in their paintings what they used to do in their leisure time.

Drawing sporting figures

It can seem difficult to draw people in action, but if you take your time, make some sketches, and look carefully, you can do it!

Body shapes
Start by drawing simple shapes to show the head, arms, and legs. Look at how the body is made up.

Try to break the body down into easy lines. Think of the shoulders as one line, the arms and legs as others.

Make sure you have made the head the right size, and check that the legs are not too long or too short.

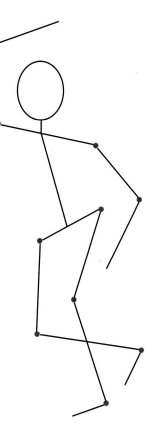

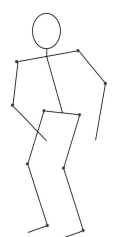

Look at where the joints are and how they move.

Once you have mastered this and the proportions look right, try drawing a different pose using the same technique.

USING INKS

WHAT YOU NEED
Thick white paper
India ink
Water
Sketchbook
Paintbrush

By adding different amounts of water to one color, August Macke could paint using different shades of blue. Why not try using inks to paint a picnic picture? Add different amounts of water to the color you choose to make different tones.

PROJECT: PAINTING WITH INK

Step 1. Make a sketch of a picnic scene on thick white paper. In your sketchbook, mix some india ink with water to make three tones of the same color—dark, medium, and light.

Step 2. Starting with the light tone, paint in the shapes. While the ink is still wet, paint in the medium and dark tones.

GALLERY

The Picnic After Sailing 1913
AUGUST MACKE (1887–1914)

WATERCOLORS
Macke usually painted in bright oil paint, but he was also skilled with watercolors.

PICNIC
Many artists at this time painted picnic scenes.

SHADES
How many different shades of blue can you see in this painting?

COLOR
The boat tells us that this was a river picnic and could be the reason Macke chose watery colors.

Although the German artist August Macke was a good student, he left school to become a painter before taking his final exams. He soon met other famous artists who decided to paint using colors full of feeling. When he died in 1914, during World War I, his friend Marc said, "With the loss of his harmony of colors, German art will become paler."

EXPRESSIONIST BOAT TRIP

The colors and shapes used by Gabriele Münter are very pleasing to the eye and can easily be turned into a collage. If you draw, cut, and paste together some simple shapes cut from cardboard or fabrics, you can make a boating scene of your own.

PROJECT: BOATING COLLAGE

Step 1. Draw your picture of a boating scene onto cardboard using simple shapes. Collect different papers and fabrics that are good colors for your scene.

Step 2. Cut out mountains, fields, and water shapes for the background and water. Arrange them on the cardboard. Add a boat and people.

Step 3. When you are happy with the arrangement, glue everything in place.

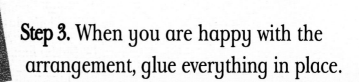

WHAT YOU NEED
Selection of paper
and cardboard
Fabrics • Pencil
Paper • Scissors
Glue

58

GALLERY

Boat Trip 1910
GABRIELE MÜNTER (1877–1962)

PEOPLE
A group of Expressionist artists used to go on vacation together each year to paint. Could this be the artists on a boat trip?

COMPOSITION
The arrangement of people, background, colors, and shapes cleverly draws your eye around the picture.

SHAPE
Münter liked to change what she saw into simpler shapes and colors.

FEELING
How does this picture make you feel? Do you think Münter liked boat trips?

When Gabriele Münter started painting in Germany, women were not allowed to put their pictures into art exhibitions with men. They were expected to stay at home and look after their families. But Gabriele spent her life painting. She particularly liked painting people. She said her work was about "self-expression," and she became a member of the Expressionist group of painters.

ANCIENT GREEK ART

Pottery in ancient Greek times was made by specially trained potters who were very skilled in using clay. Pots and bowls can be made out of papier-mâché, too, so follow the instructions and try it for yourself!

PROJECT: PAPIER-MÂCHÉ BOWL

Step 1. Ask if you may use a glass or plastic kitchen bowl, and line it with plastic wrap.

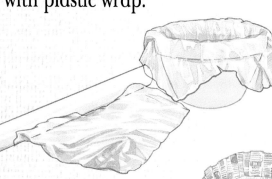

Step 2. Mix flour and water to make a soggy paste. Tear up newspaper strips, dip them into the paste, and layer them on the inside of the dish.

Step 4. Paint your bowl black or bl on the outside and terra-cotta red inside. Cut out some athletes from orange cardboard or paper and paste them around the pot.

Step 3. Make five or six layers, leaving the papier-mâché to dry between layers. When it is all dry, lift the paper bowl out carefully. You could add handles.

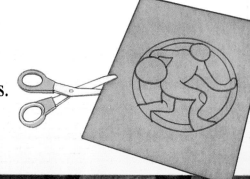

GALLERY

Greek Red-Figure Vase c510/500 B.C.
ANCIENT GREECE

OLYMPICS
Greek men and women enjoyed athletics and held the first Olympic Games. Many vases showed athletes taking part in games.

BACKGROUND
The black background of the pot was painted with a special clay that turned black when heated.

USE
What do you think this vase was used for?

This is a picture from a vase made by a Greek potter long ago. Potters would make a vase or bowl out of red clay. They would then paint the pottery with liquid clay and draw figures on the surface using a sharp tool. The heat of the kiln turned the liquid clay black, and the figures would stay red like the clay.

DETAILED ICE SKATERS

Pieter Brueghel was one of a large family of painters. He often painted cool, wintery scenes with people enjoying the ice and snow. Look for some packaging materials that could make a collage of a snowy scene. Make sure they are cool colors.

GALLERY

Winter 1622-1635
PIETER BRUEGHEL (1564–1638)

DISTANCE
The people in the front (foreground) are much bigger than those people in the distance. Yet they are all carefully painted.

ACTIVITIES
How many different activities can you see going on? Did you spot a man who had fallen into the river?

In Holland during the winter, the canals and rivers used to freeze over, and people enjoyed skating on them. Pieter Brueghel painted many scenes of children and adults spending time together having fun.

PROJECT: SNOW AND ICE COLLAGE

Step 1. Ask an adult to help you to cut out a square from styrofoam packaging and draw mountains and a lake area on it in felt pen.

Step 2. Get an adult to help you cut away the styrofoam to make the mountains and lake shapes. Use a blunt knife very carefully. Paint the sky blue and add some of the cut out mountain shapes to make more mountains. Glue a piece of shiny paper for a pond.

Step 3. The figures can be made from wire or pipe cleaners. Add skates to the feet by painting a used matchstick black and cutting it in four. Green sponge and twigs will make trees. Glue everything on to complete your picture.

3-D BALLET DANCERS

Degas made many paintings and sculptures of ballet dancers. This sculpture is full of life although it is made of metal. The same lively feeling can be given to a 3-D model made from cardboard.

PROJECT: 3-D FIGURES

Step 1. Draw a figure on thick cardboard. You may need some help to cut it out. Degas chose a ballet dancer, but you can choose any sport.

Step 2. Paint both sides of your figure. If you chose a dancer, sew a line of stitches along the top of a small piece of net and tie it around the waist.

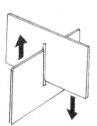

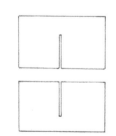

Step 3. To make a base, cut halfway through two pieces of cardboard and slot them together.

Step 4. Make a cut between your figure's feet. Slot your figure into the stand. You could make a whole troupe or a team.

GALLERY

Dancer 1896-1911
EDGAR DEGAS (1834–1917)

BRONZE
This ballet dancer is made from bronze, which is a metal. It starts as a liquid and is poured into a mold of the sculpture. When it is solid, it is polished until it shines.

dgar Degas loved to go behind the scenes at the Paris theaters to watch the ballet dancers. He would take his sketchbook, pastels, pencils, and paints and make sketches. When he returned to s studio, he would turn his sketches into beautiful sculptures and paintings.

POINTILLIST CIRCUS

WHAT YOU NEED
Colored cardboard
Pencil • Scissors
Tracing paper
Felt-tip pens
Thread
Garden stick

The circus figures here look as though they could be attached to the top of the tent by wires. A group of circus figures hanging on threads would make a moving mobile that would look good hanging in your bedroom.

GALLERY

Le Cirque 1891
GEORGES SEURAT (1859–1891)

WHITE
The white horse and edge of the ring are the first things you look at.

CURVES
The curved line takes your eye around the painting and makes you feel as if you are in a circus ring.

COLORED DOTS
From a distance it is hard to see all the dots Seurat used, but if you look closely you can see each colored dot.

PROJECT: CIRCUS MOBILE

Step 1. Copy the circus figures from Seurat's painting onto colored cardboard. You can enlarge them on a photocopier and trace them. When your figures are finished, cut them out.

Georges Seurat trained as an artist in Paris. He tried different methods of painting, but is most famous for his style called "pointillism." You can see how he put dots of color next to each other in this picture of the circus. He spent a long time arranging different colored dots to see the effect they had, and the different colors they made, before he painted his pictures.

Step 2. Use felt-tip pens to put dots of color all over both sides of the figures. Experiment with combining dots of different colors to see what new colors you can make.

Step 3. Tie threads of different lengths onto each figure and then hang them from a garden stick. Add the long thread to the stick and hang it up in your room.

MINIATURE PAINTING

WHAT YOU NEED
White fabric
Cardboard • Pencil
Fabric paint
Ink • Glue
Thick paintbrush
Thin paintbrush
Sequins

Indian artists painted small pictures that usually told a story. They painted them on paper, wood, ivory, or fabric. Today, there are many different types of fabric paints and crayons that can be used to make a picture.

PROJECT: PAINTING FABRIC

Step 1. Find a small square of white fabric. Pin it to a piece of cardboard and sketch your picture with pencil. You could use the Moghul painting as a guide.

Step 2. Color your drawing by using fabric paint or ink. Color in the main areas first, using a thick brush.

Step 3. Use a fine brush for the details. Paint a frame around the edge and glue on sequins to decorate it when it is dry.

GALLERY

Prince with Falcon
MOGHUL STYLE (BEG. 17TH CENTURY)

SPORT
What sport do you think is illustrated here? The bird is a clue.

COLOR
The man in the painting is a prince. He stands out in his brightly colored clothes.

ILLUSTRATION
This painting could have been done to illustrate a book about life in the emperor's court.

MINIATURE
Paintings like this were often very small. Fine brushes of animal hair would be used to paint the delicate lines.

Long ago in northern India, artists painted pictures of everyday life at the emperor's court. Often these were miniatures, which means the paintings were very small. The artist would tell a story in paint about important events like elephants escaping or royal hunting expeditions.

ABSTRACT BALL PLAYER

WHAT YOU NEED
Paper • Fine pen
Heavier pen
Colored pens

Picasso used all sorts of weird and wonderful shapes in his paintings. He did not paint realistic pictures that showed exactly what things looked like. You can make a Picasso-style painting by finding shapes in scribbles!

GALLERY

Ball Players on the Beach 1928
PABLO PICASSO (1881–1973)

SHAPES
Look at the person drawn in black in the background. How is this one different in shape from the main person painted?

BODY
Look at the person playing with the ball. Can you figure out which bits are arms and legs?

PROJECT: FINDING SHAPES

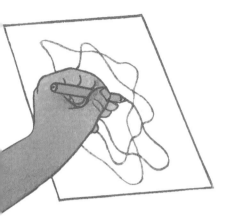

Step 1. Make some scribbles on a piece of paper using a fine pen. Take some time to look at the shapes you have made. Can you see shapes that could be made into figures or balls?

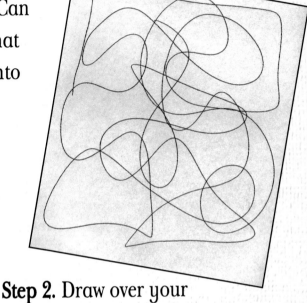

The Spanish artist Pablo Picasso changed how people saw art in the last century. He created paintings, sculptures, drawings, and ceramics that were all unusual or different from the work of other artists at that time. He used his imagination because he did not want his art to be realistic, like a photograph. When you look at one of his paintings, it may take you some time to figure out what some of the things in them are!

Step 2. Draw over your figure in a heavier pen. You could also color it in following the lines of the scribbles.

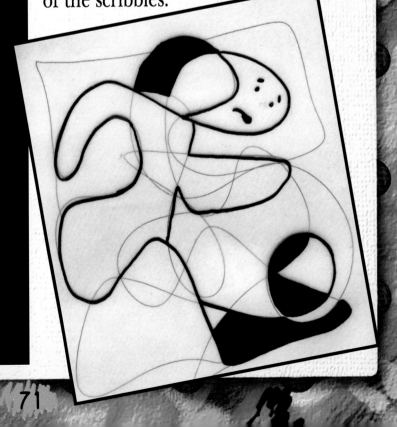

STREET SCENE IN OILS

WHAT YOU NEED
Pastels
Sketchbook
Paper • Scissors
Used matchstick
Hairspray

Renoir used oil paints for this picture of his friends enjoying a day away from work. Pastels are also effective when drawing people. Why not try drawing some Parisian dancers, as Renoir has done, or some of your friends at a dance?

PROJECT: PASTEL DANCERS

Step 1. Test your pastels in a sketchbook first to see how you can layer them or blend them. Draw a picture of people dancing. Fill in the background with different pastel shades.

Step 2. Color in the dancers. To get the effect of dappled light on the picture, scrape off some of the color with a used matchstick.

Step 3. Trim your picture and spray it with hairspray to prevent smudging.

GALLERY

The Ball at the Moulin de la Galette 1876
PIERRE AUGUSTE RENOIR (1841–1919)

COSTUME
Renoir has caught the spirit of the time by showing the details of the clothes. The hats and dresses show how Parisians dressed for a ball in 1876.

STREET LIFE
The people of Paris loved to spend their time outside in parks and squares. Here they are talking, eating, and dancing.

LIGHT
The light seems to be coming through the trees. Renoir has used a light-colored oil paint to show the effect of sunlight.

Many of Pierre Auguste Renoir's paintings show people enjoying themselves. He began work at the age of thirteen and spent his entire life painting the people and places he knew. The use of bright, fresh colors brought a cheerful touch to his work. He spent time with Monet painting outdoors and studying the effect of sunlight. During his lifetime Renoir became world famous. Today, people still travel all over the world to see his paintings.

WHAT YOU NEED
Stiff cardboard
Paint • Paintbrushes
Pencils • Scissors
Cardboard • Glue

PAINTED HORSE RIDERS

Many people enjoy riding along a beach like the figures in Gauguin's painting. They almost look as though they could jump out of the back of the picture. A 3-D effect can be achieved by cutting out horses and riders and adding them to a background.

PROJECT: 3-D HORSE RIDERS

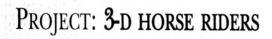

Step 1. Paint a beach background on cardboard. Draw some horses and riders on another piece of cardboard. Paint them in warm colors. Use Gauguin's picture to help you choose shapes and colors.

Step 2. Cut out the horses and riders and glue a piece of folded cardboard onto the back of each.

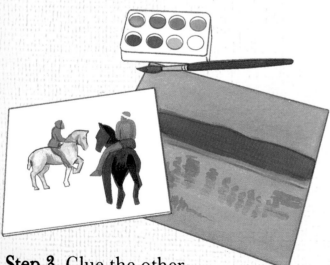

Step 3. Glue the other end of the folded cardboard to the background to finish the picture.

GALLERY

Riders on the Beach 1902
PAUL GAUGUIN (1848–1903)

TIME OF DAY
The warm but soft colors could be the early morning or evening light on the beach.

FREEDOM
The figures are not wearing many clothes and are riding their horses bareback.

BRUSH STROKES
Gauguin has used different kinds of brush strokes to blend colors together for the sky, sea, and sand.

FEELING
How does the painting make you feel? How do you think Gauguin felt when he painted it?

Paul Gauguin was born in Paris. However, he left his family and career in France to spend much of his life on the South Sea island of Tahiti. He hated city life and enjoyed living a simple life close to nature. Many of his paintings were of the tropical forests and beaches, where he loved the freedom of riding a horse. The warm colors he used show the enjoyment he had in his way of life.

SURREALIST SOCCER PLAYER

WHAT YOU NEED
Pencil • Scissors
Thick colored
cardboard
Tape • Thread
Paper fasteners

It is easy to turn a two-dimensional drawing into a movable figure if you use Salvador Dali's unusual soccer player to help you. Look closely at Dali's drawing, then draw the athlete of your choice and make a heart shape at the center.

GALLERY

Football Player c.1980
SALVADOR DALI (1904–1989)

SKELETON
This soccer player has no skin or face, and is not at all like a real soccer player.

LAYERS
It is as if Dali has gotten under the skin of the soccer player to see his movements and feelings.

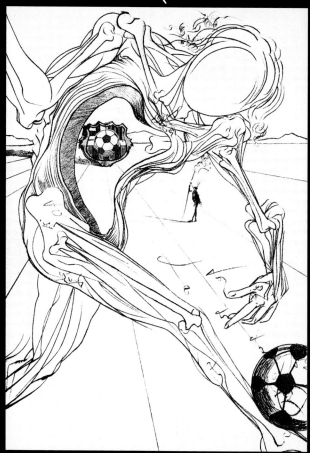

CENTER
What shape has been used to frame the ball at the center of the figure? What do you think it means?

DRAWING
You can see how skilled Dali was at drawing from the detailed skeleton.

PROJECT: MOVABLE FIGURE

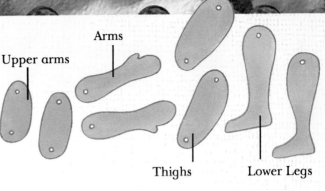

Upper arms

Arms

Thighs

Lower Legs

Step 1. Draw a head and body on thick colored cardboard. Cut out a heart shape from the chest. Tape the heart shape onto the side of the heart like a little door. Ask an adult to make holes as shown.

Step 2. Cut out two sets of arms and legs as shown above, and ask an adult to make holes as shown. Put your figure together using paper fasteners so that it moves.

After working in the United States for a number of years, Salvador Dali returned to Spain where he had been born. He was a member of the Surrealist movement of artists. His art was famous because he painted people, places, and objects in great detail, putting them together into a picture in an unusual way.

Step 3. Draw something related to your favorite sport that is small enough to hang on a piece of thread in the heart shape in your figure.

CHAPTER 4: STILL LIFE

CONTENTS

Find out how artists created wonderful works of art of everyday things, such as fruit or furniture. You can try and copy an object as accurately as you can, but you could also do something more with it.

By putting objects in front of an unusual background, for example, you can create very interesting pieces of art.

Look at how famous artists did it, and use your imagination to create your own masterpiece!

Drawing objects

A still-life picture is made up of objects that are not alive. They can be studied easily because they do not move.

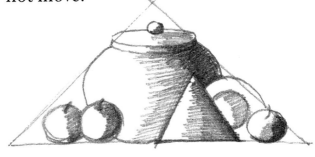

First the outline should be drawn and then the dark areas shaded, before finishing with lighter tones and highlights. This will give the object depth and make it look more realistic.

Try to arrange some objects at home into a good composition. Don't just put the objects in a line. Put some things at the front and some at the back. Look at what you have done and rearrange it until you are happy with it.

COMPOSITION

Cézanne has put together lots of objects from a kitchen to make a still-life picture. If you collect some objects from your kitchen they can be drawn using oil pastels. Don't take months to draw it like Cézanne did!

PROJECT: USING PASTELS

Step 1. Set up your still life, thinking about how you want the objects arranged. Make a light pencil sketch of your arrangement.

Step 2. Try blending and layering the oil pastels in your sketchbook. When you are confident, choose the medium shades of color and put them onto your sketch first. Remember to look carefully at the shapes you are drawing.

Step 3. After the shades of color, add the deep shadows, the shading, and the details last of all.

GALLERY

Still Life with Curtain, Jar, and Fruit Bowl 1893-94
PAUL CÉZANNE (1839-1906)

COLOR
Look how many different colors Cézanne used just to cover one small area of wall.

WHITE
Although the cloth is white, what other colors have been used?

EYE
Your eye is taken around the painting from the white cloth to see all the different objects.

LOOSE PAINT
Paint has been used loosely to give an impression of objects, not every little detail.

The French artist Paul Cézanne painted such exciting and surprising pictures that many famous artists were inspired by his work. He was not an easy friend to have as he had a very bad temper. Despite this his work was always admired. Cézanne put dabs of paint next to each other to build up a whole picture. He called this method working with a "pistol loaded with paint."

PAINTING FLOWERS

WHAT YOU NEED
Flowers • Sponge
Paper • Paint
Pastels • Hairspray
Paintbrushes
Colored Paper

Many artists including Odilon Redon have enjoyed painting flowers. Get some flowers from the garden or a florist and try out different printing and painting methods to make a colorful picture.

PROJECT: MIXED MEDIA FLOWERS

Step 1. Look carefully at the flowers you have in front of you. You could paint each flower using a different method. Start with a piece of sponge to print the petals and leaves in different colors.

Step 2. Paintbrushes and fingers can be used to dab extra colors and shapes onto the flowers.

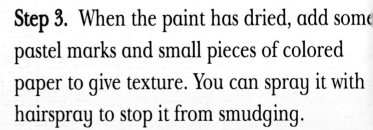

Step 3. When the paint has dried, add some pastel marks and small pieces of colored paper to give texture. You can spray it with hairspray to stop it from smudging.

GALLERY

Flowers in a Turquoise-Colored Vase c.1905
ODILON REDON (1840-1916)

BACKGROUND
The colors of the flowers stand out against the background.

VASE
This vase catches your eye, too, with its bright color.

MATERIALS
Can you see brush strokes or other marks on the painting? What do you think Redon used to paint the flowers? Look at the texture of the leaves and the petals.

Odilon Redon was often sick as a child. He became very shy and liked to hide away from people as he grew up. He did not want to be an artist like the Impressionists. He used his imagination to make black and white prints and charcoal drawings. Later in his life he found happiness with his wife and friends and began to use color. He said, "Color contains joy."

SCULPTING FRUIT

WHAT YOU NEED
Newspaper
Glue • Water
Paint • Tape
Paintbrush

Gauguin has painted the fruit in this still life to look three-dimensional. You can make 3-D fruit by using paper and glue. The pieces of fruit could then be arranged into a still life.

PROJECT: 3-D FRUIT

Step 1. Scrunch used newspaper into the shape of different fruit. Tape it together.

Step 2. Dip strips of newspaper into a mixture of glue and water. Wrap around the fruit. Leave it to dry.

Step 3. Paint each piece of fruit to look as real as possible.

Step 4. When the paint is dry, arrange your fruit into a still life.

GALLERY

Still Life with Profile of Laval 1886
PAUL GAUGUIN (1848-1903)

BRUSH
Gauguin has used a large brush and loose strokes to paint his still life.

COMPOSITION
Laval looking at the fruit draws your eye in to look at it, too.

OBJECTS
What other objects can you see on the table that Laval is looking at?

3-D EFFECT
See how shadows, tones, and highlights make the fruit look three-dimensional.

Until the age of six, Paul Gauguin lived with his parents in Peru, South America. The colors, smells, and way of life stayed with him and he always longed to return. In 1883 he decided to become a painter and traveler. Later he lived abroad and painted using very bright colors.

OBSERVATION

Leonardo da Vinci was a keen artist and he also invented things. He would carefully observe the world and draw what he saw. You can also take your sketchbook out and draw the things around you.

PROJECT: SKETCHING

Step 1. Buy some different grades of pencil, like HB, 4B, 6B, and 4H. Try them out in your sketchbook, making as many different dark and light marks as you can.

Step 2. Look around your house or backyard for interesting objects to sketch. Make sure you look slowly and carefully before you start to draw. You can write notes about what you see, too.

Step 3. Now use these sketches to make a still-life drawing, using all the different pencils you have already tried out.

GALLERY

Sketches c.1508
LEONARDO DA VINCI (1452-1519)

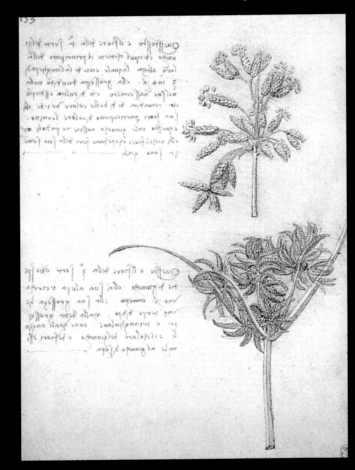

WRITING BACKWARD
Da Vinci was left-handed. In the days of writing with pen and ink, this made things difficult—as you pushed the pen forward, your hand would trail over the ink. Leonardo had a better idea. He wrote backward.

DETAIL
As there were no cameras to capture detail, Leonardo used his pencil to record plants and other objects.

OBSERVATION
Look how carefully he observed everything he wanted to paint.

Leonardo da Vinci was famous even in his own lifetime as a great artist and inventor. He was one of Italy's most gifted painters. He tried to make his paintings and drawings perfect. He made detailed studies of nature and the anatomy of the human body. He made sketches of airplanes, helicopters, and many other machines that were not even invented when he was alive.

COLLAGE

WHAT YOU NEED
Magazines
Scissors • Glue
Cardboard

Magritte did many paintings of everyday objects in places you wouldn't expect to see them. If you look for some pictures of places and objects in magazines, you can make a surrealist picture, too.

PROJECT: **SURREALIST COLLAGE**

Step 2. Put your chosen object into the frame so that you can still see some of the view around it.

Step 1. From a magazine, choose a picture of a room, landscape, or seascape. Glue it to a piece of cardboard. You can make a frame to go around it. Find a picture of an interesting object that will fill the cutout view, but that looks really strange. Try out a few first.

GALLERY

The Listening Room 1958
RENÉ MAGRITTE (1898-1967)

SIZE
Why do you think the apple is so large? Is it the only thing you look at in the picture?

VIEWER
What size does this picture make you feel?

APPLE
This apple looks so real you feel you could take a bite out of it.

LISTENING
Can you figure out why he called this picture "The Listening Room?"

By the age of 12, Magritte was going to painting classes. Later, he did a four-year art course in Brussels, Belgium, where he lived. He had many interesting ideas and said he wanted to express his thoughts in paint. He found the world a wonderful and mysterious place and, like Salvador Dali, became a surrealist painter. He often painted ordinary objects in strange places, such as a large apple in a small room.

SCULPTURE

WHAT YOU NEED
Clay • Paint
Paintbrush

Henry Moore made sculptures using simple shapes. He often used clay to make a model of a large sculpture he was planning. Clay would be a good material for you to make a 3-D shape in the style of Henry Moore's work.

GALLERY

Oval with Points 1968-1970
HENRY MOORE (1898-1986)

VIEW
Can you see how the shape makes a frame around the view through the center?

SURFACE
What material do you think Moore used? The surface catches the light.

SIZE
This shape is larger than life and fills a great deal of space.

POINTS
The two points almost touch and draw your eye to the center of the shape.

PROJECT: SCULPTING IN CLAY

Step 1. Take a lump of clay and make it soft by rolling, shaping, and squeezing it. Mold it into the shape of a number eight.

Growing up in Yorkshire, England, gave Henry Moore a great love of the countryside. He studied art in Leeds and London, but it wasn't until after World War II when Moore was in his forties, that he found fame. He continued to work until he was 88 years old. His main work was making enormous sculptures in bronze and stone that he placed in the countryside.

Step 2 . Use your fingers to create two different-sized holes in the shape.

Step 3 . When the clay dries, you can paint it with bronze-colored paint or leave it clay-colored.

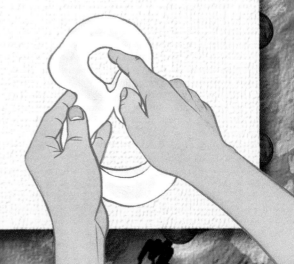

MAKING A COLLECTION

Schwitters used tickets, stamps, postcards, advertisements, and other objects to make his works of art. If you collect things that you like, you can make an arrangement of them and they will remind you of good times.

PROJECT: CONSTRUCTION

Step 2. When you have finished, glue the objects into the box. You could hang it on the wall.

Step 1. Paint the inside of a shallow box a bright color—for example, red. Divide the box up with cardboard strips, which you can also paint. Collect things that you like or that are special to you and arrange them in the sections of the box. Why not add your initials so your box is made personal?

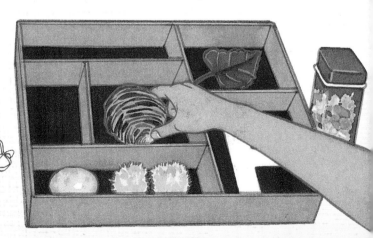

GALLERY

Merzbild P 1930
KURT SCHWITTERS (1887-1948)

MATERIALS
How many different kinds of material can you see in this picture?

ARRANGEMENT
Do you like the way Schwitters has arranged his materials, or would you have done it differently?

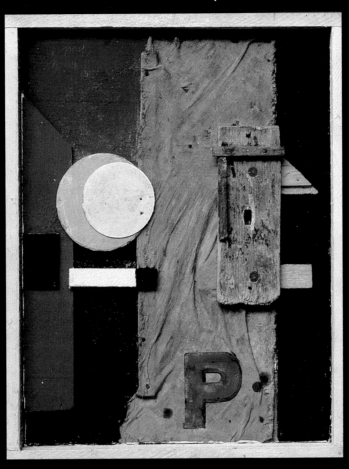

FEATURES
One of the main features in this construction is the keyhole. The letter P is also very eye-catching.

Born in Germany, Kurt Schwitters later moved to Norway and then England where he stayed. His art is called abstract because he arranged objects at random without meaning. He collected different materials together and arranged them to make a picture or a construction. He gave this art the new name of Merz because no one had ever done art like it before.

CUBISM

WHAT YOU NEED
Colored Paper
Black Felt Pen
Scissors • Glue
Pencils • Paint
Paintbrush

Picasso looked at the different planes and angles of an object and then painted it in a cubist style. If you draw an object then cut it up and rearrange it, you can make a cubist picture.

PROJECT: CUBIST COLLAGE

Step 1. Use the objects in Picasso's picture or some you have chosen yourself. Draw them onto colored paper using a black felt pen.

Step 2. Draw and paint a background of a window onto a piece of cardboard. This will frame your image.

Step 3. Cut up the objects you have drawn using straight lines. Arrange them onto the background and glue them in place when you are happy with how it looks.

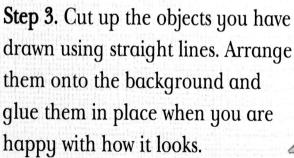

GALLERY

Guitar and Table in Front of a Window 1919
PABLO PICASSO (1881-1973)

WINDOW
Picasso often used an open window as part of his painting to give it a sense of space.

CUBISM
Painting objects or people by using straight lines and geometric shapes is called Cubism.

OBJECTS
What other objects can you see in this picture?

COLOR
Picasso has chosen to use a range of colors for this picture. Are they warm or cool colors?

From an early age Pablo Picasso showed his talent at drawing. He spent his whole life making many different kinds of art, and produced more art than any other modern artist. Many people found his work hard to understand, but this did not stop him from fascinating the world with his unusual works of art.

WHAT YOU NEED
Scissors • Shoe Box
Paint • Paintbrush
Cardboard • Glue

WORKING IN 3-D

Van Gogh lived a simple life, but his room looks attractive with its bright colors. You can bring van Gogh's bedroom to life by making it in cardboard in three dimensions. When you have done that, you could also make a 3-D picture of your own room. Remember to clean it up first!

GALLERY

Vincent's Bedroom at Arles 1889
VINCENT VAN GOGH 1853-1890

BRUSHSTROKES
These thick brush strokes look just like a wooden floor.

SHADOWS
There are no shadows in the room as the shutters are closed, keeping out the light.

PROJECT: 3-D BEDROOM

Step 1. Cut the front off an old shoe box or other small box. Paint the walls and floor to look like van Gogh's bedroom.

Step 2. Make a bed and chairs out of cardboard. Make sure they fit into the box. Paint them the same colors van Gogh used.

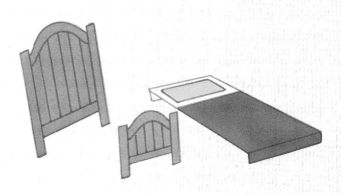

For several years, van Gogh lived in the south of France. This is the bedroom in the house he shared with Paul Gauguin. The two artists worked together and they often argued as well, especially about who should clean the house. This painting shows how neat van Gogh could be, and is a record of how he lived.

Step 3. When the furniture is dry, fold the bottom of the legs under. Arrange them in your room, and when you are happy with their positions, glue them to the floor of the box.

ABSTRACT ART

WHAT YOU NEED
Paper • Pencil
Glue
Paintbrush
Paint
Printing Ink

Fernand Léger used abstract shapes in his work. He would paint them in bright colors. If you use bright colors, you will see how the different shapes that you paint stand out.

PROJECT: ABSTRACT SHAPES

Step 1.
Make a sketch of some shapes. You can use cylinders like Léger. Use a tube of glue to draw lines of glue over the pencil lines. Leave it until it is dry and really hard.

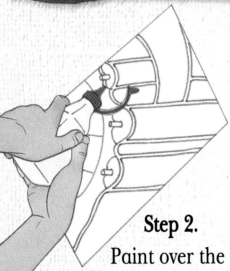

Step 2.
Paint over the glue lines with dark paint or printing ink. Before the paint dries, press a piece of paper onto it.

Step 3. Peel the paper off carefully and let it dry. When it has dried, paint bright, clear colors into the spaces.

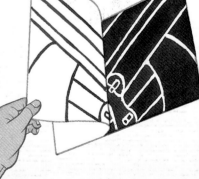

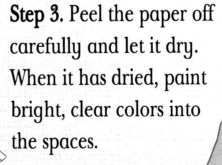

GALLERY

Cenpa 1953
FERNAND LÉGER (1881-1955)

COLOR
Léger used clear, bright colors so that different parts of his painting stood out from each other.

CYLINDERS
The cylinder is often seen in Léger's work as many machines have this shape.

BLACK LINES
Black lines around the shapes on Léger's painting make it look like a stained glass window.

MACHINES
What kind of machine do you think has been painted here?

Fernand Léger was brought up on a farm in northern France. His father died when he was a small boy and as a young man he fought in World War I. Both events affected him a great deal. He often seemed angry, but he was kind underneath. The world was using more and more machines, and Léger used color, shape, and pattern to show the new "machine age" in which he lived.

PATTERN AND COLOR

WHAT YOU NEED
Paper Plate
Paints
Paintbrush

Aboriginal art uses patterns and warm colors to decorate all kinds of objects. This art uses color and pattern to great effect. You can decorate a plate in the same style.

PROJECT: DECORATING A PLATE

Step 1. Take a paper plate and some bright natural colored paints.

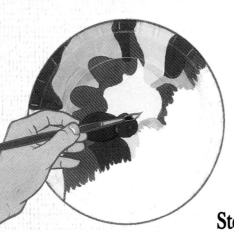

Step 2. Start by painting the background of the plate. Divide it up into sections of bright colors. Let it dry.

Step 3. When it is dry, you can add the pattern on top. Use black and white paint to stand out against the bright colors you have used. You could make your pattern a flower or another object that you might see in nature.

GALLERY

Aboriginal Artifact
ABORIGINAL ART (PRESENT DAY)

FABRICS
Today Aboriginal designs are often used to decorate fabric that can be made into clothes.

PATTERN
This pattern is exactly the same as those that have been used by Aborigines for thousands of years.

DOTS AND SPOTS
The dot or circle was used a great deal in Aboriginal pattern making.

Aborigines have lived in Australia much longer than anyone else. From earliest times they used color to decorate their bodies, rocks, wooden and clay pots, spears, boomerangs, and shields. Crushed rocks and flowers were used as paints, while feathers and chewed bark served as brushes. Today in some parts of Australia, this same style is used to decorate objects used in everyday life.

Chapter 5: Animals

Contents

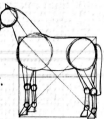

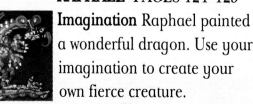

A lot of artists like to make sculptures, paintings, or drawings of animals, from wild tigers, to pet cats, or even goats!

Learn to look carefully at different animals. What shape are they? Do they have fur, or feathers?

Look at some famous artists' work for inspiration, then create a piece of art of a pet, animal, or a make-believe dragon!

Drawing animals

It may seem difficult to draw animals, but if you take your time, do some sketches, and observe carefully, you can do it!

Body shapes
Start by drawing simple shapes to show the head, body, legs, tail, and ears.

Proportion
Make sure you have made the head the right size, and check that the legs are not too long or too short.

 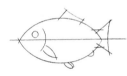

 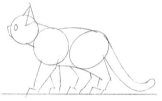

Fur, hair, and skin
Does the animal have fur, hair, skin, or unusual colors? Find out how you will draw them by trying out some ideas in your sketchbook.

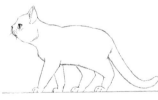

Finishing touches
Once you have the size and shapes right, you can start to fill in the details and add color.

REALISTIC DRAWING

WHAT YOU NEED
Pencil • Paper
Ruler • Compass
Colored Pencils

Horses were George Stubbs's favorite animals. He studied them for ten years, doing hundreds of drawings of them. He made these into a book tha artists and veterinarians used in their work. You can practice drawing a horse by using simple geometric shape

GALLERY

Horse and Rider 1771
GEORGE STUBBS (1724 – 1806)

CONTRAST
A careful use of light and dark shades of color bring the horse to life. Stubbs made the horse darker than his master so you look at the horse first.

REALISTIC
Look at the horse's muscles. They look so real that the painting could almost be a photograph.

George Stubbs was born in Liverpool, England. He taught himself to draw, paint, and make etchings. He spent years studying horses and became a famous horse painter. Rich people paid him to paint them in their huge grounds, by their big houses, with their favorite horses.

PROJECT: DRAWING

Step 1. Look carefully at Stubbs's horse. Draw a square with two diagonal lines crossing it. Draw a large circle in the top left corner and a small one in the top right.

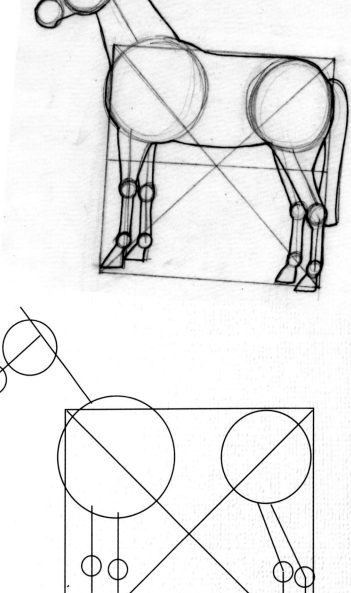

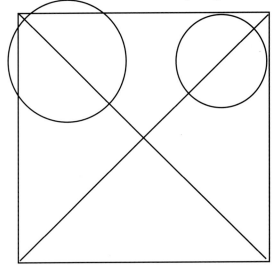

Step 2. Now add some straight lines from the circles for legs. Put small circles for the knee and ankle joints. The head and neck can be added by using straight lines and a large and small circle.

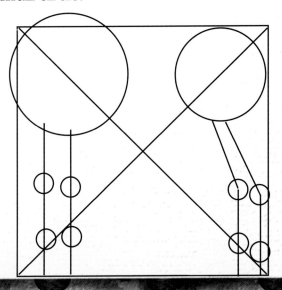

Step 3. You can finish the drawing by adding the body, neck, ears, legs, and tail to the lines and circles. When you have practiced drawing a few horses you can add color to them.

ROMAN MOSAIC

Mosaics were used by the Romans to decorate walls, floors, and pavements. This dog was found in Pompeii, Italy. It is a warning sign saying, "Beware of the Dog." Why not make your own mosaic of your pet or any interesting animal?

PROJECT: PET MOSAIC

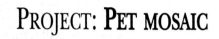

Step 1. Draw a simple outline of your animal on cardboard. Use a photograph or picture from a magazine or book to help you.

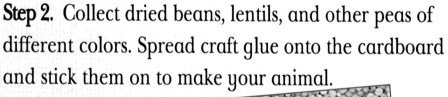

Step 2. Collect dried beans, lentils, and other peas of different colors. Spread craft glue onto the cardboard and stick them on to make your animal.

GALLERY

Beware of the Dog AD 79
POMPEII MOSAIC

MATERIALS
Mosaics were usually made from many small, colored stones, tiles, or marble. This one was made from marble pieces.

WARNING
The dog looks as fierce as the artist could make it, to scare people away.

COLORS
Marble is never found in very bright colors, so the tones used for this dog are natural: red, white, and gray.

DECORATION
Mosaics were used to decorate palaces and churches in ancient times.

This mosaic was discovered in the remains of Pompeii long after Mount Vesuvius had erupted in AD 79. It was probably made to lie in the sidewalk outside a wealthy person's house. It would have acted as a warning to passersby to beware of the dog; it would also warn thieves to keep away!

ASSEMBLAGE

WHAT YOU NEED
Craft Glue • Foil
Tape • Scissors
Cardboard • Knife
Ruler

Picasso used different materials he may have found in his workshop or yard to make his goat. Look around your home for cardboard, tape, and foil to make a three–dimensional model like this.

PROJECT: 3–D MODEL

Step 1. Cut an oval shape out of cardboard. Draw two lines across the center with a knife and ruler (this is called scoring; ask an adult to help). Fold along the lines.

Step 2. Cut three rectangles out of cardboard. Score three lines on each and fold to make the neck and two pairs of legs. Copy the shape on the left, score along the lines, and fold for the head.

Step 3. Use lots of tape to join all of the pieces together. Cut the bottoms of the legs and fold outward to help the model stand.

Step 4. Ears and horns can be cut out from the leftover cardboard. Bend the horns into a curve and tape them onto the goat's head.

Step 5. Finish by gluing scrunched-up aluminum foil all around the goat and adding a tail and beard.

GALLERY

Goat 1950
PABLO PICASSO (1881 – 1973)

MATERIALS
Picasso used plaster, wood, and clay to make his goat. How many different textures can you see in the sculpture?

STRUCTURE
A wire structure would have been made in the shape of a goat so that a plaster of Paris mixture would stick to it.

WOOD
The goat is standing on an old piece of wood. Other pieces of wood have been used to make the surface of the animal look more interesting.

POSE
Can you see the goat is looking up with a perky tail and ears? How would you describe Picasso's goat?

Through his paintings, sculpture, drawings, and ceramics, the Spanish artist Pablo Picasso changed how people saw art in the twentieth century. He used many different kinds of materials to create his works of art. He was always making something unusual, right to the end of his life. Sometimes he would make sculptures by using bits and pieces he found. This is how he made this lively goat.

ATTENTION TO DETAIL

WHAT YOU NEED
Paint • Pencil
Orange Stick
Printing Block
Clay / Play Dough
Paper

Dürer has drawn his hare in great detail, looking carefully at the fur, eyes, ears, and nose. You can make a print of your own pet using Dürer's hare to help you. Try to put in as many details as you can.

PROJECT: ANIMAL PRINT

Step 1. Make a sketch of your pet using a pencil and paper. Put in as many small details as you can. Look carefully at the fur, face, and tail.

Step 2. Use a sharp pencil or orange stick to draw your pet onto a printing block. You can use flattened-out clay or play dough instead.

Step 3. Cover the printing block with paint. Try out the print on a scrap of paper first. Press it firmly down onto the paper and rub over the back of it. Pull it away carefully. When you are pleased with it you can print onto your best paper.

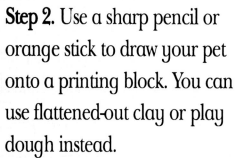

GALLERY

Young Hare 1502
ALBRECHT DÜRER (1471 – 1528)

DETAIL
A very fine brush was used to put in all the small details. You can see almost every hair and whisker on the hare.

FEATURES
Can you see how realistic this hare is? The nails look very sharp, the eyes bright, and the ears listening.

PAINTING
Dürer usually made prints. He probably did this painting in his spare time for pleasure.

MOVEMENT
Although the hare is sitting still, Dürer has made it look very alert, as if it will leap off at any minute.

Albrecht Dürer was born in Germany and trained to be a goldsmith with his father. He soon got bored and went off traveling. In Italy, he found he enjoyed drawing, printing, and painting, and he quickly became famous for his book illustrations. He loved showing every small detail in his work. He did this with his prints as well as his paintings.

CAVE ART

WHAT YOU NEED
Oil Pastels /
Charcoal Pencil
Sketchbook
Pencil • Thick
Cardboard • Acrylic
Paints
Sand

Long ago, people painted the walls of caves with pictures of animals and sometimes people. The paintings were probably thought of as magic and were painted in special places away from where people lived.

PROJECT: WALL DRAWING

Step 1. Find a piece of thick cardboard. Mix some sand with white and pale yellow acrylic paint. Cover the cardboard with the paint to make it look like the wall of a cave.

Step 2. Sketch some outlines of animals in your sketchbook. Copy two or three onto your homemade wall, using a black oil pastel or charcoal pencil.

Step 3. Shade each animal with yellow and reddish brown, which were the colors used by cave artists.

GALLERY

Horse 17,000 BC
LASCAUX CAVE PAINTING

SURFACE
You can see that this horse has been drawn on a wall by looking carefully at the surface. Can you see the cracks, scratches, and marks there?

LINE
It is easy to see the outline of this horse even though it is very old. The artist would have used a sharpened stick dipped in dark earth.

EYE
Which way do you think this horse is looking? Perhaps it is wondering what will be coming up behind it.

MAGIC
Ancient people were often afraid of things they did not understand. They thought their paintings made a magic that would help them.

This horse is part of a 100-foot-long gallery of prehistoric cave paintings at Lascaux in France. The only colors used were made from powdered rock and soil. White, green, and blue were not used because they could not be made. The paintings were often made in dark caves, and this helped to protect them so that we can still see them today.

CLAY SCULPTURE

WHAT YOU NEED
Clay • Paints
Brushes
Craft Glue
Plastic Knife

Henry Moore's owl is a very simple shape, but you couldn't mistake it for any other animal or bird. He started making his owl in plaster and finished it in bronze. You can make an owl by molding clay and using simple shapes and textures.

PROJECT: CLAY OWL

Step 1. Soften some clay in your hands and form it into an owl shape. Push two holes through the clay for its eyes by using your finger or a plastic knife.

Step 2. You can add wings, a beak, and feet. Use different tools to make a rough texture on the clay like feathers.

Step 3. When the clay is dry, paint the owl and cover it with watered-down craft glue to varnish and protect it.

GALLERY

Owl 1966
HENRY MOORE (1898 – 1986)

TEXTURE
Can you see different marks on the surface of the owl? Do they make you think of feathers, a beak, and feet?

OBSERVATION
Before he started on his final sculpture, Henry Moore made many sketches and smaller plaster models.

ry Moore was still working until he was almost ety. He lived in England all his life. His huge res of people, animals, and shapes can be seen countryside and many different cities all over orld. This owl is one of his smaller pieces and is careful observation, skill, and love of wildlife.

JUNGLE PAINTING

Rousseau liked to paint animals in jungles with large leaves and colorful flowers. You can put a tiger in a jungle by cutting shapes out of scrap magazines and hiding the tiger behind them.

PROJECT: TIGER COLLAGE

Step 2. Collect gold, green, and brown colors from magazines. Cut out leaf and tree shapes. You can make some colorful flowers, too.

Step 1. Draw a tiger and color it with chalk pastels. Cut it out.

Step 3. Put the tiger onto a dark background and arrange the leaf, tree, and flower shapes around and on top of the tiger. Make sure you can still see it!

Step 4. Glue the shapes on when you like the arrangement. You have made a jungle collage.

GALLERY

Exotic Landscape With Tiger 1907
HENRI ROUSSEAU (1844 – 1910)

LEAVES
How many different leaf shapes can you see? Rousseau studied tropical plants in Paris so he could paint them.

COLOR
The main color used by Rousseau is green. What effect does this have on the other colors he has used?

CAMOUFLAGE
Is it easy or difficult to see the tiger among the leaves? What is the tiger hiding from?

ANIMALS
There are two other animals watching and waiting to see what will happen. Can you see them?

When he retired from an office job, Henri Rousseau began to paint. He taught himself, and to his surprise soon became famous. Picasso liked his paintings and gave Rousseau a big party to celebrate his work. For this jungle painting, Henri Rousseau went to a zoo in Paris to study the tigers.

UNDERWATER DREAM

WHAT YOU NEED
Thread • Tape
Crayons
Cardboard • Fine
Stick • Scissors
Craft Glue
Sticks
Straws

In his Fish Magic picture, Paul Klee used a mixture of paints to get the effect he wanted. His fish have interesting faces and skin patterns. They look as if they are hanging on strings, like a mobile. It is easy to make fish like Klee's.

PROJECT: FISH MOBILE

Step 1. Color a pattern onto two pieces of cardboard using bright crayons. Don't worry if the colors go on top of each other.

Step 2. Color over both patterns with black crayon. On one, use a fine stick to scratch five or six fish shapes just through the black. Put patterns on each fish.

Step 3. Cut them out, tape a piece of thread onto the back. Glue them onto the other piece of cardboard facing back to back.

Step 4. Cut them out and scratch a pattern onto the back of each fish. Tie the fish onto two sticks or straws. Use thread and straws to hang your mobile.

118

GALLERY

Fish Magic 1925
PAUL KLEE (1879 – 1940)

DREAM
Klee wanted this painting to look like a dream while also seeming like a fish tank.

TIME
This fish tank has a sense of timelessness, yet in the center is a clock. It has stopped at the exact moment Paul Klee finished this painting.

COLOR
The colors Klee has chosen to use are similar to those you might see at the bottom of a lake or the ocean.

STRANGE OBJECTS
A moon, a clown, and a vase are floating in this picture. What else can you see that is unusual?

Most of the important art galleries of the world have some of Paul Klee's paintings. He was born in Switzerland, but did most of his work in Germany. He liked to use his imagination and created many pictures that had a dreamlike feel to them, like this one. He used color, patterns, and shapes to express his ideas.

AFRICAN ANIMAL MASK

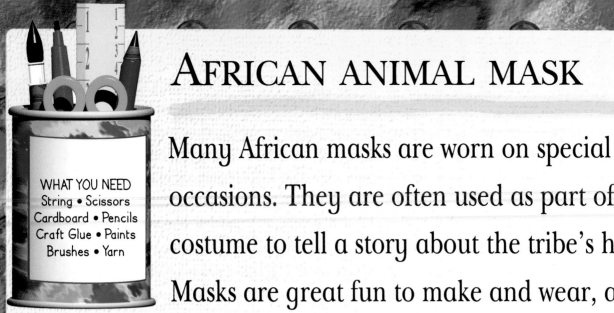

Many African masks are worn on special occasions. They are often used as part of a costume to tell a story about the tribe's history. Masks are great fun to make and wear, and can be made quite easily.

WHAT YOU NEED
String • Scissors
Cardboard • Pencils
Craft Glue • Paints
Brushes • Yarn

PROJECT: ANIMAL MASK

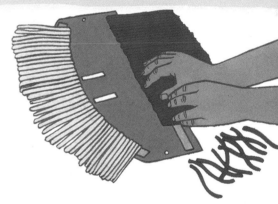

Step 1. Cut out face and horn shapes from dark cardboard. Punch a hole on each side just above the ears, and cut out eye slits. Draw on a patterned face and paint it with a medium brush.

Step 2. Turn the face over when it dry. Add yarn fringe to the bottom and cardboard strips to the top.

Step 3. Stick the horns on the front of the mask. Fold the cardboard over the horns like a fringe. Tie string through the holes and fasten over your face.

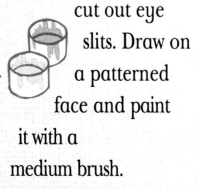

GALLERY

Shangaan Dancer in Costume (Present day)
VICTORIA FALLS, ZIMBABWE

PATTERN
Triangular lines over the eyes make the face look angry or fierce.

FEELINGS
Masks were made to make people watching feel sad, frightened, or happy. How does this mask make you feel?

ANIMAL
What animal do you think this mask is supposed to be? What makes you think this?

COLOR
Only brown, white, and black are used on this mask. It helps to make it look more dramatic.

African masks are made out of many different materials and are used for ceremonies such as weddings, funerals, or harvest. Sometimes wood is used, and feathers, straw, and paint are added as decoration. This mask is an animal with horns, and may be part of a hunting story.

WHAT YOU NEED
Inks • Pen
Brush • Pencil
Chalks • Cardboard
Sketchbook

OBSERVATIONAL DRAWING

Gwen John did many paintings of cats, and enjoyed using brush and ink with some white chalk highlights. Inks come in many different colors and can be used with brushes, pens, or a stick. Draw a portrait of your favorite cat. Use chalks to add color and give the cat some features.

GALLERY

Cat 1904–08
GWEN JOHN (1876 – 1939)

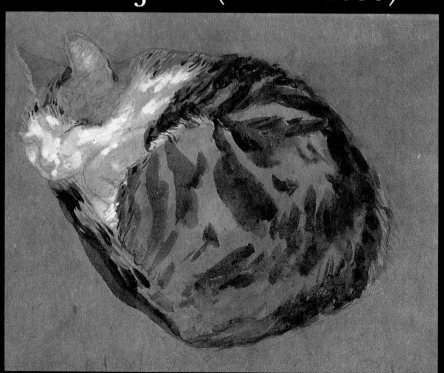

DETAIL
Just a few brush strokes and chalk marks make this little sleeping cat come to life.

BACKGROUND
Gwen John has used the brown color of the paper to play an important part in her drawing of her cat. Choice of surface can make all the difference in a work of art.

PROJECT: INK AND CHALK CAT

Step 1. Sketch your chosen cat standing, asleep, and walking. Choose your favorite pose and draw an outline of it on colored cardboard or paper.

Step 2. Choose an ink that matches your cat, and go over your outline with pen or brush. You can water the ink down to make it lighter. Add details of pattern in the fur and markings on the face and tail. When it is dry, use colored chalks to add details like eyes, nose, whiskers, and colors in the fur.

Paris was the city Gwen John chose to live in after she had finished her art training in London. She wanted to get away from her father and her famous artist brother, Augustus. As she grew older she spent her life quietly, doing beautiful pale drawings and paintings of people, her cat, and parts of her house. She did not look after herself very well, and died of starvation when she was 63.

IMAGINATION

Raphael's painting tells the story of St. George fighting the dragon. Raphael used his imagination to make his dragon. He has made it look very wicked and dark. You can make a mixed media dragon that looks lively and colorful.

PROJECT: MIXED MEDIA DRAGON

Step 2. Paint in the patterns and shapes on the dragon's skin, wings, and face. Paint a bright color around the outline of the whole dragon.

Step 3. Cut up some silver, gold, and shiny paper and stick it onto the dragon. Sequins, buttons, shiny wrapping paper, and thread can be added, until you have a very bold dragon.

Step 1. Draw the outline of an imaginary dragon on dark cardboard with a light chalk or pencil line.

GALLERY

St. George Fighting With The Dragon c.1505
RAPHAEL (1483 – 1520)

DISTANCE
The dragon and St. George stand out, while the background fades into the distance in pale blues and greens.

WOMAN
St. George has rescued this woman from the evil dragon. Can you see how Raphael has made her look soft and delicate?

DRAGON
Raphael used different tones of black and white to make the dragon's skin shine and gleam in an evil way.

HORSE
Why do you think the horse is white? It certainly stands out in the center of the painting.

When Raphael was eleven, his father died. He then went to work in a studio to learn to become a painter. He became one of Italy's most famous artists. Best of all, he liked to paint the Holy Family and saints. In this painting he is showing how good overcomes evil, from the popular story of St. George saving the young woman from the terrors of the dragon.

GLOSSARY

ABSTRACT
A work of art that is not an exact copy. Shape, color, and pattern are used to give a feel of the subject.

ASSEMBLAGE
A work of art made up of a collection of selected objects.

CANVAS
Thick cotton or linen fabric stretched over a wooden frame, used instead of paper for painting on.

CARICATURE
Comic picture of a person made by drawing exaggerated chin, nose, eyes, hair, or body.

CARVING
Making a shape, pattern, or design out of material like wood or stone by cutting with a sharp tool.

CHARCOAL
Slightly burned twigs or sticks that turn black and are used by artists for drawing.

COLLAGE
The placing of different materials on a backing to make a pattern or picture.

COMPOSITION
The way different parts of a painting are arranged to get the effect the artist wants.

CONSTRUCTION
Materials fitted together to make a work of art.

CONTRAST
Colors, shapes, or patterns

that look very different when they are put side by side.

CUBISM
An art movement using distorted shapes to show objects from more than one angle.

ETCHING
Acid is used to cut out a picture into a piece of metal. Ink is then put on and a print is made of it.

EXPRESSIONISTS
A group of artists who use color, line, and shape to show emotion rather than to make pictures that look like the real world.

FABRIC
Material or cloth made by weaving.

FOCAL POINT
The most important part of a painting that stands out from everything else and draws the eye to it.

FOREGROUND
The part of the view that is at the front of a picture.

GROTESQUE
A face or design that is made to look comically strange.

HIGHLIGHT
Part of a painting or drawing that has been made lighter to show where the light is reflected.

IMPRESSIONISTS
Group of French artists who used light and color in their paintings to give an impression of what they were looking at.

MARBLE
Hard rock that comes in many patterns and colors and can be cut, carved, and polished.

MIXED MEDIA
Many different kinds of materials used by artists to create unusual works of art.

MODEL
A smaller than life, three-dimensional sculpture of an animal, person, or object.

MOLDING
To change the shape of a material, like clay, into a new, more imaginative shape.

MOSAIC
A picture made on a wall or floor by pressing glass and stones into cement.

OBJECT
Something that is not alive but can be seen or touched.

OBSERVATION
Looking closely at something so that a more accurate work of art can be made.

PALETTE KNIFE
A trowel-shaped knife used to put paint on and to scrape it off the canvas.

POINTILLISM
Dots of paint put close to each other, which the eye turns into blocks of color.

PORTRAIT
A picture of a person or people that can be made using any materials.

PRINT
A picture made by pressing paper onto a marked surface.

REALISTIC
A work of art that is made to look exactly like the real world.

RELIEF
A carving made on the surface of a piece of rock, stone, or wood.

SCULPTURE
An object made from hard or soft materials that can be looked at from all sides.

SEASCAPE
Artwork of a view of the sea.

SHADE
A darker or lighter tone of the same color used to make a picture have more depth.

STILL LIFE
Objects grouped together to make a picture.

SURFACE
The outside of something that you can see and feel.

SURREALISM
Art that brings together unusual objects and imaginary places that would not be seen in the real world.

TEXTURE
The feel or look of the outside or surface of something.

THREE-DIMENSIONAL
An object or work of art is three-dimensional if you can walk around and look at it from all sides.

TONES
The many different shades or tints of a color.

INDEX

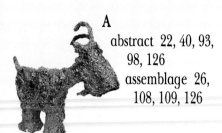